# FLYING SCOTSMAN IN AMERICA
## AMERICA
### THE 1970 TOUR

RICHARD HINCHCLIFFE AND
BILL WAGNER

AMBERLEY

# Acknowledgements

Thanks to all who have made this book possible. While we would like to think that our memories of events fifty years in the past would be sufficiently indelible to let us write this book unaided, many of the specific details, dates, and sequences of events came from Bill Wagner's contemporaneous hand-written notes and George Hinchcliffe's memoir *An Obsession with Steam*. Thanks also to Penny Vaudoyer, Chris Wragg, Bill Gamble and Joe Petric. We hope you have as much fun reading about our summer with *Flying Scotsman* as we had putting it in writing.

First published 2023

Amberley Publishing
The Hill, Stroud
Gloucestershire, GL5 4EP

www.amberley-books.com

Copyright © Richard Hinchcliffe and
Bill Wagner, 2023

The right of Richard Hinchcliffe and Bill Wagner
to be identified as the Authors of this work has
been asserted in accordance with the Copyrights,
Designs and Patents Act 1988.

ISBN 978 1 3981 1521 7 (print)
ISBN 978 1 3981 1522 4 (ebook)

All photographs by Bill Wagner unless otherwise
indicated.

British Library Cataloguing in Publication Data.
A catalogue record for this book is available from
the British Library.

Typesetting by SJmagic DESIGN SERVICES, India.
Printed in the UK.

# Contents

# Introduction

There are few accounts of *Flying Scotsman*'s tour of North America from 1969 to 1972. Various narratives cast it as 'failed', a 'disaster', or a 'dark hour', and admittedly, for owner Alan Pegler it was a literal misfortune as he filed for bankruptcy. In 1954 he was the man who brought the Ffestiniog Railway back to life and who 'saved' *Flying Scotsman* from the scrapyard in 1963. He was a railway enthusiast's hero and a man used to success. However, Pegler had 'no regrets' about the American tour and had enjoyed driving his engine when this was not possible in the UK. In retrospect, given the reception from the American and Canadian public, how she'd travelled thousands of miles across the continent and then was heroically rescued as creditors closed in to seize her, *Flying Scotsman*'s extraordinary North American escapade reinforced her legendary status as the world's most famous steam locomotive.

This book is a pictorial record of the 1970 tour – from Slaton, Texas to Niagara Falls, Ontario – the middle tour and the lengthiest of the three that took her down, up, and across that great continent. There are three principal characters: there's *Flying Scotsman*, a foreign engine in a strange land, approaching her fiftieth birthday. Then there are the authors of this book – British, thirteen-year-old Richard Hinchcliffe, and, just leaving his teens behind him, Illinois railfan Bill Wagner. They now share their memories with you. So, this is also their story; Bill and Richard's excellent adventure as part of the retinue of the world's most famous steam train. It was to be the year of their lives.

There are some great pictures of *Flying Scotsman* in this book, but the text also documents some of the remarkable crew. Richard's father was George Hinchcliffe, the railway heritage pioneer who managed *Flying Scotsman* for about thirty years from the 1960s into the 1980s. George was a great character, endlessly inventive, with a quick wit and temper. He arranged the engine's coaling, watering and maintenance on the first tour in 1969 when, with her nine-coach train, she toured from Boston to Houston. The carriages were full of British exports like Johnny Walker whisky and Pretty Polly tights. The companies themselves did well, exhibiting to buyers and expanding their markets but the train itself was over staffed, the organisation having failed to fully understand how the 'circus', as it came to be called, might make sufficient money to make the tour profitable. When *Flying Scotsman* got to Washington DC, Alan Pegler asked George to take over full management of the train. They saved some money by sending a few staff home. But George asked for his wife Frances to come over to help him, as she was his assistant back in the UK, and their son Richard came too. It was the first time either of them had flown in an airplane. To her horror, Frances was asked to manage seventeen young, British tartan-skirted ladies that sold the public souvenirs and entry tickets. Meanwhile, Richard became the train's 'official' messenger boy. At Houston the tour ended and the train was stored over winter at Slaton, Texas, in a disused Santa Fe railroad roundhouse.

Slaton is a small town of about 7,000 people, located in the Texas panhandle just a few miles south of Lubbock. Six weeks were spent there getting the 1970 tour ready. New exhibits were fitted out in exhibition carriages while details of the route became finalised. The train crew all stayed at the El Lora Motel. George and Frances were at the hub of the organisation in room number seven, also their office, getting the train ready. Richard was with them, again taking time off school. They often didn't notice where he was or who he was with. One boiling hot afternoon he stumbled into room eight by mistake. A Texan drawl asked him to 'Come on in.' Richard found a blonde woman in complicated white underwear lying on the bed. The voice came from a bare-chested cowboy wearing a Stetson hat. 'Whoaaa!' said Richard, 'wrong room!'

The full crew of Brits, many of whom were on a 'working holiday' were now enjoying the Slaton hospitality. Like Richard, they would have equally bizarre cultural experiences as the tour went on. Davina Flint was Alan Pegler's personal assistant, as she had been on the 1969 tour. Nick Lord and Ron Hawkes, British railway enthusiasts, were the train managers and Simon Puser was the accountant. Peter Boht, the bartender, served Watney's Red Barrel and joked with customers in the observation car's Fireman's Rest bar. He would also travel ahead of the train to arrange publicity. The engine crew consisted of three drivers and two firemen. Nat Gould, Arthur Houghton, and Gordon Pugh would take turns driving *Flying Scotsman* across the continent while Bill Brand and Alan Wappat spent the summer shovelling coal into the firebox. Les Richards was the chief locomotive inspector, and Harry Mason was the fitter responsible for the engine's upkeep. Gordon, Nat, and Les brought their wives along on the adventure. May Gould, Ethyl Pugh, and Ena Richards now replaced the seventeen tartan-skirted ladies helping Frances sell souvenirs. Two young local Texan sisters, Shauna and Mary Elaine Snow, were volunteers who travelled with the train for the entire tour. They were the daughters of a Fort Worth businessman who secured their places on the train to give them 'life experience'. As the summer progressed, they became romantic interests for the eligible men on the tour. Rounding out the crew were Bill Wagner and Randy Imfeld, who had come to Slaton to install an exhibit on the train and stayed to become the tour's semi-official photographers and odd-job men. George managed the whole of the 'circus' while Alan Pegler, playing the part of an eccentric British millionaire, drove the engine, underwrote the finance and kept an eye on George.

Bill Wagner's route to Slaton wasn't as straightforward as Richard's. He grew up in Dixon, Illinois, and had become interested in railroads when he was Richard's age. There was a very active group of young railfans in northern Illinois, who had spent their high school years photographing trains throughout the country. Primary interests were passenger trains and steam locomotives. Bill was well aware they were seeing the last days of extensive long-distance rail travel in the country and that they'd already missed the last days of steam. Their weekend photography trips usually centred on major cities like Chicago, St. Louis, Kansas City, Cincinnati, or St. Paul where you could still find passenger trains. Occasionally, railroads like the Burlington and the Grand Trunk would run weekend excursion trains pulled by steam engines. They'd ride or chase them, whenever and wherever they were scheduled.

Bill had never heard of *Flying Scotsman* until the news broke about her 1969 trade tour from Boston to Houston. To say that he was intrigued is an understatement – here was a passenger train pulled by an exotic and historic steam engine. And to make matters even better, there were plans for a once-in-a-lifetime event in Anniston, Alabama, where three steam engines would meet – *Flying Scotsman*, and two American steam engines pulling excursion trains. Bill just had to be in Anniston.

Like Richard, Bill's first airplane flight was due to *Flying Scotsman*. That was the only realistic way for him to travel the 700 miles to Anniston, since he was a full-time college student without a car on campus. The 'Steam-O-Rama' was everything he'd expected it to be, and *Flying Scotsman* was the star of the show. When the day of chasing steam trains with his friends, from Atlanta to Anniston to Birmingham ended, he never expected to see *Flying Scotsman* again.

Even though he'd been away at college, he was still going on weekend trips with his railfan friends from high school days. Many of the guys in the group eventually turned their interest in trains into their lifelong careers: Craig Willett became an engineer driving trains for Amtrak. Mike Schafer and the late Jim Boyd each authored numerous railroad books and edited many railroad publications.

Jim Boyd was the unquestioned alpha railfan and elder statesman of the group. In early 1970, he somehow procured half of one of the display cars on the *Flying Scotsman* tour

Sunday, 2 November 1969. Left to right: LNER *Flying Scotsman*, No. 4472 (4-6-2), Savannah & Atlanta No. 750 (4-6-2), and Southern Railway No. 4501 (2-8-2), are all under steam and in charge of passenger excursion trains. The 'Steam-O-Rama' featured an impromptu whistle-blowing competition among the locomotives. The engineers on No. 750 and No. 4501 were musicians and entertained the crowd with a worthy fanfare from each whistle. Unfortunately, *Flying Scotsman*'s engine crew had let the fire die down during the long stop in Anniston. Even with some frantic last-minute shovelling of coal, there was not enough steam to produce more than two 'peeps' from its Gresley peanut whistle.

Bill Wagner and Randy Imfeld arrive in Slaton with the NWI exhibit. *Flying Scotsman* and the rest of the tour train are still in the roundhouse, being prepped for the beginning of the 1970 tour in less than a week. A host of other characters including Richard Hinchcliffe and his parents make up the team getting the train ready and finalising the route. And the summer lies ahead.

train for the local railroad club (North Western Illinois Chapter of the National Railway Historical Society). The group created an exhibit called 'The Railfan' that described the things railfans did in pursuit of their hobby. It featured a small model railroad diorama, photographs from around the country, original artwork, and collectibles such as timetables, cloth headrests, locomotive builder's plates, and even dinnerware. The central artwork of the exhibit was a sculpture created from a railroad spike: a sort of stylized railfan. Joe Petric, who has also kindly contributed some photographs to this book, was another member of the group.

By June, the exhibit was completed and ready to be installed on the *Flying Scotsman* tour train. The problem was that the exhibit was in northern Illinois and the tour train was cocooned 1,200 miles away in the Santa Fe roundhouse in Slaton, Texas.

That's when Bill's path crossed with *Flying Scotsman* again. Bill was an unemployed college student with no plans or obligations for the summer. His friend from high school days, Randy Imfeld, was likewise unemployed and without any plans. So, they volunteered to drive the exhibit to Slaton. Between them, they had enough money for gas (and film) for at least a one-way trip. And, once they got the exhibit installed on the train, money-making opportunities might turn up. It was worth taking the chance.

# Slaton

In which *Flying Scotsman* emerges from the roundhouse, Alan Pegler solves a coaling problem, and Bill sells his blood.

Monday, 8 June. *Flying Scotsman* and the entire tour train had spent the winter in Slaton's Santa Fe Railroad roundhouse. Here, the administration car and one of the exhibition cars are getting ready to see daylight in 1970 for the first time. By the time Bill arrived, *Flying Scotsman*'s crew members had already started cleaning up the train. They were nice enough to let him and Randy sleep in compartment C of the administration car. The seats were comfortable enough as beds but the Texas heat made the airless roundhouse a miserable place, even at night.

Tuesday, 9 June. One by one, the tour train cars are pulled from the roundhouse onto the turntable. Later that day they'll be assembled into the train itself and moved to the Santa Fe station.

*Above*: The train's exhibits will be displayed in four converted LNER pigeon vans used in the 1960s for transporting racing pigeons. A fifth van is used to store souvenirs and supplies.

*Right*: Bill Brand (fireman) and Nick Lord (train manager) fill up an exhibition car axle box with oil. This maintenance had to be done every day the train moved – seventy-two axle boxes to check and top-up with oil. American railroads have lineside hot-box detectors and the train will be stopped if an axle box overheats due to insufficient lubrication.

By evening, the train has been fully assembled. A Santa Fe GP-7 will pull it the half mile from the roundhouse to the station.

Figures of 'beefeaters' advertising Beefeater gin overlook the interior of the bar in the observation car. The tour train stands outside of the Santa Fe depot, which had been a Harvey House restaurant during the heyday of railroad travel. The Fred Harvey Company operated a chain of restaurants, hotels, and other hospitality venues at railroad depots throughout the western United States. This former Harvey House had not been used as a station since passenger services through Slaton ended in the late 1960s. The Santa Fe had turned it into a storeroom for overflow documents from their adjacent business office. Today, in 2023, it has been restored to its Harvey House condition and is a bed-and-breakfast hotel.

Sunset in Slaton. The observation car was built in 1918 as an LNWR ambulance coach but was converted into a Pullman car in 1921, then rebuilt as a bar car in 1937. It became an observation carriage in 1947 for the *Devon Belle*. Richard remembers travelling on it in 1964 from Inverness to Kyle of Lochalsh in pouring rain. Incongruously, here it is in the baking Texas sun. After America its adventures continued, being bought and repatriated to the Swanage Railway and restored at Derby Railway works.

A quiet night after a hectic day. The nineteen-member UK crew will spend the next four days installing exhibits and getting equipment ready for a summer of constant travel. The electrics are arranged by Ron Hawkes (train manager) for exhibits to be ready for the public as quickly as possible. The record was three minutes. Bill and Randy spent the time ingratiating themselves with the UK crew, ferrying them back and forth to the El Lora Motel, fetching their lunches from the Red Arrow Cafe, and doing most of the train's heavy lifting work. They also spent a morning selling their blood at the Lubbock Blood Bank. It was their first successful money-making venture of the summer.

*Left*: Saturday, 13 June. *Flying Scotsman* is finally under steam and ready to make her grand emergence from the roundhouse.

*Below*: *Flying Scotsman* shows off the 'Americanization' required to tour the country: a headlight, a bell, and a bright red pilot (cowcatcher). The bright red pilot would become a source of contention later in the tour. There's such a thing as looking 'too Americanized'.

*Flying Scotsman* will be the last railway locomotive to be serviced in the roundhouse, which would be demolished within a year.

View of *Flying Scotsman* from the turntable pit.

View of *Flying Scotsman* from the roof of the roundhouse. The roundhouse turntable at Slaton was built to accommodate Santa Fe's giant Mallet-type locomotives. Even with two tenders, No. 4472 fits easily with several feet to spare. Bill and Randy had a special appreciation of the Santa Fe maintenance facility (seen in the upper left). It contained a shower, which they needed to use at least once a day. For obvious reasons, the crew also appreciated it.

The Santa Fe GP-7 won't be needed to pull *Flying Scotsman* down to the station. She'll steam there under her own power once her tender has been loaded with coal.

There's *Flying Scotsman*. There's a pile of coal. And there's a problem. The hired front-end loader could not reach high enough to fill the tender. Alan Pegler (owner of *Flying Scotsman*) and Les Richards (chief inspector) search for a solution. In 1968, Les had been one of the locomotive inspectors on No. 4472's famous recreation of the non-stop run between London King's Cross and Edinburgh.

Solution: First use the front-end loader to scrape up some earth to build a ramp, and then fill the tender.

*Above*: Alan Wappat (fireman) spreads the coal as Les Richards supervises.

*Left*: A fireman's work is never done. After coaling, Alan Wappat wipes the tender down before *Flying Scotsman* steams to the station. Note the roll-up cigarette and the handkerchief 'Gumby' hat keeping off the sun and the coal dust.

View from the roof of the station as *Flying Scotsman* and her tour train are reunited, with miles and miles of the Texas panhandle stretching off into the distance.

All polished up, *Flying Scotsman* is ready to greet visitors in the morning. White flags on American railroads indicate that the train will be running as an 'extra' when the tour begins in two days. By this time the UK crew had accepted Bill and Randy as part of the team, assuming they'd continue their informal taxi service and help sell tickets and souvenirs after the tour began. The crew occasionally gave them a few dollars here and there for food and gas, so they decided to stick with the train as long as their money held out. As far as they knew, they'd be the only two Americans joining the nineteen Brits as full-time crew members.

Sunday, 14 June. The train is opened free of charge in recognition of Slaton's great hospitality. George Hinchcliffe (general manager) oversees the operation from *Flying Scotsman's* pilot, while Alan Pegler looks on from the driver's seat. Ron Hawkes is below the cab while driver Nat Gould's wife May stands at the end of the first tender. It wasn't just opening for business that made the day memorable. It turned out that Bill and Randy would not be the only Americans on the full-time crew. Two sisters, volunteers Mary Elaine and Shauna Snow from Keller, Texas, arrived in mid-afternoon. They would also remain with the train throughout the summer.

Visitors have to keep an eye out for passing freights, like this one led by a Santa Fe F-7. Stairs to the exhibits were always placed on the station side of the tracks whenever the train was open for business. It wasn't just the locations of the stairs, but all the other procedures needed to welcome guests on the train got their shake-downs that day – ticket sales and collection, electric generator, the route through the exhibits, visits to *Flying Scotsman's* footplate, and souvenir sales and restocking. There's more to operating a 'travelling circus' than initially meets the eye.

*Right*: When the train is open for display, Alan Pegler spends as much time as he can greeting visitors on the footplate. One reason he brought *Flying Scotsman* to America was so that he could often drive his own locomotive, which wasn't allowed in the UK. In 1971, even though he was running out of money, he would carry on with the tour of America, all the way to San Francisco, negotiating for another government-backed trade mission and unsuccessfully trying to get more funding. His family did not approve of him 'playing trains' and were in no position to bail him out financially.

*Below*: *Flying Scotsman*'s last night in Slaton. The 1970 tour would begin in the morning. Bill had a full tank of gas and a fresh roll of film and was ready for the first day of a 3,400-mile chase that would end in Niagara Falls, Ontario, Canada.

# Slaton to Waco

In which an exhibition car develops a hot-box, the crew learn about bad trackage, and Richard gets a taste of American train chasing.

Monday, 15 June. Sunrise in Slaton on a beautiful clear Texas morning.

The deserted Santa Fe rail yard behind *Flying Scotsman* indicates how the fortunes of railroading in Slaton have changed over the years.

With fire in the firebox and water in the boiler, *Flying Scotsman* comes to life in front of the mission-style Santa Fe office building adjacent to the station.

Finally under way, *Flying Scotsman* passes Slaton's deserted Santa Fe maintenance facility half a mile down the tracks. The roundhouse where the train had spent the winter is just out of sight to the right. Richard is also chasing the train, not with Bill and Randy but with legendary railroad photographer Emery J. Gulash. His Oldsmobile station wagon was faster and more accommodating than Bill's Opel. In the back, Emery J. had two Panner Bolex 16 mm movie cameras with tripods, two Pentax single-lens reflex cameras, two Yashica twin-lens reflex cameras and a cool box full of beer and soda-pop.

Only 25 miles into the trip, the train made an unexpected stop in Post to repair a hot-box on one of the exhibition cars. After the train stopped in the centre of town, Bill and Randy found themselves helping with repairs. A crowd looked on as they fetched the required tools and supplies from the storage car. Their strong backs were turning out to be handy. Bill remembers this was where he first really felt like he was actually part of the enterprise. 'What an ego trip!'

At Post, the flat south plains of the Texas panhandle give way to the buttes, mesas, and escarpments of west Texas. With repairs complete, the train hustles out of town en route to Brownwood, where it will tie up for the night.

Yes, there is some water in west Texas. Here's *Flying Scotsman* crossing the Double Mountain Fork of the Brazos River in Justiceburg. The historical monument in the foreground highlights the legend of the Coronado expedition of 1540–1542, where the Spanish explorers found fresh water in the Brazos and were saved from dying of thirst.

With not even a telephone pole in sight, it's definitely new countryside for *Flying Scotsman* as the train is watched by far more rattlesnakes and scorpions than people.

More water in west Texas, but this time it's a man-made reservoir just outside of Lawn. *Flying Scotsman* had already made a mid-day stop in Sweetwater, but Bill and Randy were not there to help with the souvenir sales. They'd managed to lose the train somewhere outside of Snyder, and mistakenly assumed they were behind it when they finally found the tracks again. After they figured out they'd made a second mistake, they backtracked and eventually spotted the train just before it passed Lawn Lake.

Last views of the west Texas landscape as *Flying Scotsman* arrives in Coleman.

Coleman, with a population of about 5,500, is one of the larger towns that the train passes through on the day's run to Brownwood.

Arriving at Brownwood, *Flying Scotsman* whistles for a grade crossing on the northwest side of town. The ticket and souvenir sales in Brownwood went quite smoothly after the rehearsal in Slaton. After closing, the UK crew (and the Snow sisters) hosted some local dignitaries and news reporters in the observation car's Fireman's Rest bar. This would become a ritual at the train's one-night stops.

*Flying Scotsman* spends a quiet night in Brownwood's Santa Fe station. It looks like a quiet scene. However, there's enough water in the Brownwood area to support a healthy cricket population, and they decided to serenade the train. Between the heat and the crickets, Bill and Randy found it wasn't a pleasant night for sleeping in the administration car.

Tuesday, 16 June. Today's route will take *Flying Scotsman* from Brownwood to Temple. The train is passing through Copperas Cove, a small town adjacent to the huge U.S. Army base at Fort Hood.

At Temple, the Santa Fe trackage from Brownwood merges onto the main line linking Houston to Ft. Worth.

The train will arrive at the Santa Fe station in Temple in a few minutes and spend the night there before transferring onto the Missouri, Kansas, Texas (MKT or 'Katy') Railroad in the morning. Although Bill, Randy, and the Snow sisters were the only full-time volunteers, there was an ongoing string of short-timers who would spend a day or two with the train as it travelled across the continent. Bill and Randy would often taxi them out to dinner while the more presentable crew members hosted the nightly soirees in the Fireman's Rest. In Temple, volunteer Bob Fleuret treated them to pizza in exchange for a ride to the restaurant. 'It sure beat ketchup sandwiches.'

Wednesday, 17 June. *Flying Scotsman* has just left Santa Fe trackage and backed down onto the Katy. The Katy's finances were such that 'deferred maintenance' had become a way of life, as indicated by the weed-infested right-of-way on the railroad's main line. Weeds were the least of the Katy's problems. Rotten ties (sleepers) and washed-out ballast ensured that the rails themselves would frequently dip and sway. Here, both the administration car and the first exhibition car are noticeably misaligned with the rest of the train.

The train gingerly pulls onto the Katy's main line en route to Waco. It will stay on Katy trackage for the next week, all the way to Kansas City, Missouri. Randy had decided to ride the train that day from Temple to Waco, so Bob Fleuret chased with Bill. That's Randy leaning out of the door on the observation car. He managed to make it to Waco without getting seasick.

*Flying Scotsman* is open for an unscheduled hour or two in Troy. Richard recalls being stopped by signals and that a Texan who had been expecting the train asked if the exhibits could be opened. George Hinchcliffe agreed, but asked how the residents would know about it. Meanwhile was there any water? The man turned out to be W.A. Freeman: the mayor, fire captain, and also owner of the local TV, radio, and newspaper. The best part of a thousand people visited the train while the fire department filled the tender with water.

Leaving Troy behind, *Flying Scotsman* rolls slowly toward Waco beneath a clear sky and with a clear stack. The Katy railroad was concerned that cinders might start a fire on the trackage's dry weeds, so the firemen tried to keep smoke to a minimum.

After two days of relatively high-speed running on the Santa Fe, the train is slowed to a much more sedate pace on the Katy's poor trackage. *Flying Scotsman* has become more like the *Crawling Scotsman*. Richard recalls this gave Emery J. Gulash an opportunity to set up all his cameras. Rare swing arm level crossings were his favourite locations.

The Katy dispatched a track car to follow directly behind the train from Temple to Waco. Its mission was to put out any fires that might be caused by errant cinders. The track car had no difficulty keeping up. Staying on the tracks was a bigger challenge.

# Waco to Kansas City

In which *Flying Scotsman* derails, it's over 100 degrees in the shade, and Richard gets caught trying to steal a coke.

Wednesday, 17 June. Arriving in Waco, the train is passed by a mile-long southbound Katy freight led by five GP-40s. Les Richards, Nick Lord and Harry Mason (fitter) keep an eye out for problems with the track, walking alongside *Flying Scotsman* as the train slowly approaches Waco's Katy station.

Even though the train approaches the station at walking speed with multiple eyes watching for potential problems, *Flying Scotsman* derails her trailing Cartazzi axle box wheel-set when switched down the wrong track. George Hinchcliffe recalled that a worse set of wheels to be 'off the road' could not be imagined as they do not pivot and only have sideways play. The American crew on the footplate was quick to try and put things right but, before George could stop it, they'd replaced the white metal bearings on the left-hand side, reversed the train back and re-railed the locomotive. This was exactly the wrong thing to do because their actions caused the journal of the axle to be badly scored.

A scored or scarred journal would result in a hot bearing so repairs had to be made. The wheel-set would have to be taken to the nearest railroad shop 70 miles away in Cleburne. In order to remove the trailing truck for shipment, the locomotive is first separated from the corridor tenders.

*Flying Scotsman's* missing trailing wheels are on the way to Cleburne for repairs. What was scheduled to be a one-night stop in Waco has turned into a two-day stay. Richard's father was awakened at midnight by a phone call from Clebourne. The diameter of the wheels was too great to fit in their lathe. They had a 30-ton press, could they press the wheels off for the first time since the loco was built? What choice was there? By 10 a.m. the next day, the wheels were back and, by mid-afternoon, they were installed and the engine crew raised steam.

Visitors to the train's exhibits in Waco don't have the chance to step onto *Flying Scotsman's* footplate.

*Flying Scotsman's* corridor tender. The door on the left opens into a narrow corridor that runs the length of the tender and allows access to the locomotive from the administration car.

Waco is a division point on the Katy, where trains change crews. Railroaders can stay at hotels like this between assignments. Bill and Randy had two nights to spend in Waco and were tempted by the 50 cent cots. But frugality won out. Instead, they spent their money doing laundry at an air-conditioned laundromat and, as usual, slept in the non-air-conditioned administration car. Richard remembers the temperature reached a high of 104 Fahrenheit. He was left to his own devices as his parents were busy with the derailment aftermath. As he was now addicted to soda-pop and desperate for a drink, he tried to abscond with a bottle of coke from the Katy Railroad office. He was told to scram.

Friday, 19 June. Repairs complete, *Flying Scotsman* is once again on the move heading to Dallas. Bill rode the train for the first time while Randy chased from Waco to Dallas in Bill's car. Unlike the Dutch doors on American passenger cars, the full-length doors in the LNER Pullmans allowed Bill to extend at arm's length for photographs.

Near Waxahatchie, the train sits on a siding as a southbound Katy freight disappears into the distance. The trackage to the left is the Katy's main line. It's unclear how the lone GP-40 got that close to the observation car. Unlike the track car that had followed the train from Temple to Waco, it had not been following *Flying Scotsman* to watch for wayward cinders.

Arriving in Dallas Union Station. To make up for the lost day in Waco, the train would only spend one night instead of two in Dallas. It was the first stop in a big city on the 1970 tour and the train was greeted by reporters from all the local newspapers and TV stations. The Snow sisters proved to be excellent (and popular) hostesses conducting the press through the displays. The crew heard the result of the UK general election with Ted Heath elected as Conservative prime minister. Harold Wilson's previous Labour government put money in *Flying Scotsman's* first US tour. The new Tory government would not be interested.

*Left*: Sunday, 21 June. *Flying Scotsman* leaves Texas behind, crossing the Red River into Oklahoma north of Denison, where the train had spent the previous night after leaving Dallas.

*Below*: Near Durant, the train stretches out against a backdrop of Oklahoma hills.

*Flying Scotsman's* mid-day stop in McAlester is only a few minutes away.

The train crosses an embankment holding back the North Canadian River somewhere between McAlester and tonight's stop in Muskogee. When the train left McAlester, Bill noticed his car had a slow leak in one of the rear tyres. He also had a bald tyre in front and no spare. He was hoping to make it to Kansas City, where there would be time to have some tyre repairs done.

This is 1970 with the Vietnam War raging on. The train is frequently hailed by young spectators displaying Churchillian 'V' for victory signs co-opted as peace symbols. At trackside Bill tries his best to imitate one, with limited success.

Monday, 22 June. *Flying Scotsman* passes a grain elevator in Oklahoma's agricultural country. It won't be long before the train enters Kansas, en route to Parsons. Once again, Randy rode the train while Bob Fleuret chased with Bill. Bob would be leaving the train when it arrived in Kansas City the next day.

Looking down the rail as *Flying Scotsman* is about to split a pair of 'searchlight' signals.

The Katy's trackage is noticeably better here as *Flying Scotsman* lays down a plume of smoke crossing a bridge in southern Kansas.

In *Wizard of Oz* country, *Flying Scotsman* rolls toward Parsons. It might be Kansas but Dorothy would surely not expect a British Gresley Pacific steam locomotive.

Both of the Katy's main lines and several branch lines intersect in Parsons. The town is also a division point, and home to the Katy's main workshops. But even here, the track is in terrible shape. Bob Fleuret was in disbelief about the state of the Katy's tracks. He and Bill held their breaths as *Flying Scotsman* entered Parsons and approached the station.

All's well that ends well. The train safely arrives at the Katy station in downtown Parsons as a crowd waits to visit the exhibits and buy souvenirs.

Tuesday, 23 June. A way-freight from Canute led by a Katy GP-7 works the yard at Parsons as *Flying Scotsman* steams toward Kansas City. The train will be on display for a week at Kansas City Union Station. Randy drove Bill's car again while Bill rode the train.

View from the Fireman's Rest bar as the train passes a Katy freight at Olathe. Even though there was plenty of room in the Pullmans and observation car, the Interstate Commerce Commission (ICC) didn't permit the public sale of tickets to ride between cities as the train had vacuum brakes, not air brakes. However, much later, when it was too late, George discovered the ICC regulations only stipulated a fail-safe system, which applies to both vacuum and air brake systems. An opportunity for some much-needed income was missed – only crew members and invited guests like members of the press were allowed on these runs.

As a Kansas City Union Terminal SW-1200 switch engine idles nearby, *Flying Scotsman* enters the station's train shed. The station waiting room was built to cathedral proportions in 1914. It was notorious for being the location of the 'Kansas City Massacre', a 1933 shootout where four policemen were killed by a gang involving Charles Arthur 'Pretty Boy' Floyd.

# Kansas City Through St. Louis

In which *Flying Scotsman's* cowcatcher gets repainted, the crew take a riverboat ride, and Richard fakes an illness.

Tuesday, 23 June. *Flying Scotsman*, Bill and his car pose for a portrait just east of the train shed at Kansas City Union Station. After driving onto the platform to drop off crew members, Bill found that two of his tyres had finally failed him. And no spare. Luckily, the security guards at the station were friendly – they let him leave the car overnight until he could get the tyres repaired. He spent the following morning rolling first one tyre then the other to a downtown service station to have them patched.

Wednesday, 24 June. Missouri Pacific's *Missouri River Eagle* passenger service to St. Louis is ready to depart behind an E-8 as *Flying Scotsman* looks on. In 1965, there had been thirty to forty passenger trains passing through each day. By 1970, the station only hosted eighteen. The advent of nationalized passenger service through the creation of Amtrak was less than a year away.

Saturday, 27 June. With a week to spend in Kansas City, the crew are finally able to sell tickets and souvenirs on a regularly scheduled rotation. Art Flocker (volunteer, in Schweppe's apron) sells cold drinks from an ice-filled garbage can to Simon Puser (accountant) as Peter Boht (bartender and publicist) and Davina Flint (Alan Pegler's personal assistant) look on. Bill remembers that one of Art's hobbies was collecting ladies' scarves. He kept his collection in a suitcase that never left his side. Whenever a lady with a scarf walked past, Art would explain he was a collector, open his suitcase to show he was serious, and ask for hers. More often than not, she would agree.

Tom Leaton (volunteer) sells tickets underneath the station's train shed. He joined the train the previous day in Kansas City, and will stay until Chicago. Bill and Richard are still in touch with Tom. He was an Oxford Rhodes Scholar and visited the Hinchcliffes in 1971. The usual staffing assignments were one or two drivers or firemen on the footplate, one person selling tickets, one collecting them at the exhibit entry, one selling cold drinks from the garbage can, and three or four selling souvenirs. George was always around to supervise. Meanwhile, Peter would hold court in the Fireman's Rest. The bar wasn't open to the public, but crew members would often stop by for a libation or two.

The souvenir sales table in Kansas City. Left to right: Nick Lord, Shauna Snow, May Gould, Ena Richards, Mary Elaine Snow, and George Hinchcliffe. Only four were actually selling souvenirs – Nick and George are 'supervising'. Richard would often help his mother, Frances, out on the souvenir stall by going into the store car to get more stock. One hot day he was so bored he faked fainting so he could go back to the hotel and watch any of the 200 different TV channels. Staffing requirements for souvenir sales reached their peak in Kansas City. By the end of the tour, generally only two people were needed.

Monday, 29 June. Last night in Kansas City. The train will be heading to St. Louis in the morning.

*Flying Scotsman* enjoys a quiet moment before the nightly parade of Santa Fe transcontinental passenger trains descends on the station. She'll watch six pass through before sunrise: *Texas Chief*, *Super Chief*, and *El Capitan* travelling in both directions on their way to and from Chicago and destinations in the west.

All's quiet at the Fireman's Rest bar in the observation car after the last invited guests have departed. Well, it wasn't always quiet. If the day's invited guests happened to include an attractive young lady, Peter was always more than willing to keep the bar open a bit later than advertised.

*Above*: Tuesday, 30 June. After a week of inactivity, *Flying Scotsman* stretches her legs on the Norfolk & Western (N&W) as she passes the 'searchlight' signals in Excelsior Springs Junction, Missouri. She'll remain on N&W trackage all the way to Chicago.

*Right*: *Flying Scotsman* rounds a curve beneath the Missouri Farmer's Association agricultural co-op's grain elevator in Salisbury.

En route to the mid-day stop in Mexico, Missouri, *Flying Scotsman* races through a Missouri forest. Several members of Bill and Randy's railroad club including Jim Boyd, later to become editor of *Trains* magazine, drove to Mexico to chase the train to St. Louis. Jim met Alan Pegler there for the first time. Jim was appalled by *Flying Scotsman's* un-British-like bright red pilot (cowcatcher), and started lobbying Alan to paint it black. Also joining the entourage from the Illinois chapter was Joe Petric, whose excellent photos supplement this book alongside Bill's.

The order boards – the 'signals' by the side of the Martinsburg depot – indicate that there are no train orders to be caught by the crew as *Flying Scotsman* rolls toward St. Louis in the late afternoon. Randy had decided to ride the train again, so Bill had room for a passenger on the afternoon chase. Shauna asked if she could come along. To Bill's pleasant surprise, her idea of new 'life experiences' included chasing trains.

Late afternoon has become early evening as *Flying Scotsman* approaches the end of the day's run to St. Louis.

Wednesday, 1 July. The massive train shed at St. Louis Union Station covers thirty-two tracks. They're mostly unused, and *Flying Scotsman* has the gigantic facility almost entirely to herself.

*Flying Scotsman* will spend the next week on display in the depths of the station. The heat plus the humidity made sleeping in the administration car for Bill and Randy even more miserable than the nights in Texas. Luckily, fellow railfan Jim Trousdale had recently moved from northern Illinois to St. Louis and offered to let them stay at his apartment while the train was in town. (Photo: Joe Petric)

Saturday, 4 July. *Flying Scotsman* awaits Independence Day visitors before daybreak. The red pilot will be gone when night falls again. Alan Pegler agreed to repaint the pilot as long as the train crew didn't have to do the work. Jim Boyd and his crew were happy to fill the void. (Photo: Joe Petric)

Jim Boyd examines *Flying Scotsman's* pilot to understand the scope of the project. (Photo: Joe Petric)

Mike Schafer, future author and editor of numerous railroad books, joins Jim Boyd in planning how to approach the repainting as Richard Hinchcliffe looks on. (Photo: Joe Petric)

*Above*: Alan Pegler gives his final approval to the repainting project, with Richard Hinchcliffe, hands dirty from helping clean the pilot, sitting above the buffer beam. See also the final picture in this book. (Photo: Joe Petric)

*Left*: *Flying Scotsman* shows off her new black pilot in the afternoon sunshine. Big improvement! Jim Boyd gets credit for not only noticing that the red pilot was an aesthetic problem and offering a solution, but also convincing Alan Pegler that he was right.

Driver Gordon Pugh, firemen Alan Wappat and Bill Brand, and volunteer Robin Russell seem to like the results of the repainting.

After the repainting, Jim Boyd and one of his paint crew join Harry Mason and Arthur Houghton (driver) in the Fireman's Rest to celebrate and hear some of their railway reminiscences. (Photo: Joe Petric)

*Left*: Sunday, 5 July. The entire crew of *Flying Scotsman* is treated to a ride on the Mississippi riverboat *Admiral*. Arthur Houghton takes part in the festivities as Harry Mason looks on.

*Below*: Peter Boht, enjoying the afternoon boat ride on the *Admiral*. Peter always enjoyed the company of the ladies, although here he may have been out of his usual comfort zone.

Monday, 6 July. St. Louis Union Station was the largest train station in the world when it was built in 1894. The adjacent fountain designed by Carl Milles represents the meeting of the Mississippi and Missouri rivers.

The Milles Fountain and Herb Fuller, outside of St. Louis Union Station. Herb Fuller was a photographer and the son of the owner of Green Bay's National Railroad Museum, Harold Fuller. Harold, along with the late Nelson Blount, was a backer of the American tour, which would bring *Flying Scotsman* to his museum for a month. When the train would eventually leave Green Bay, Pullman *Isle of Thanet* would be staying behind at Harold's museum. Here in St. Louis, Herb's father asked him to take some pictures of the station and the famous fountain. Herb took his job seriously. Pictures of the fountain weren't good enough. He had to get pictures from inside the fountain.

*Left*: Standing outside of St. Louis Union Station, Mary Elaine Snow watches Herb Fuller's wet photographic adventure. The tour is less than a month old, but already she and her sister Shauna have made indelible impressions on the whole crew, especially the eligible men, who include Nick Lord, Ron Hawkes and Bill and Randy.

*Below*: *Flying Scotsman* spends her last night under the train shed before the next day's run to Chicago. That's a Railway Express Agency (REA) car on the Norfolk & Western train ten tracks away. REA provided package delivery service across the country in the days before FedEx. With passenger trains disappearing, REA finally declared bankruptcy in 1975.

Arthur Houghton inspects and services *Flying Scotsman* as steam is raised in the boiler.

View from a signal bridge as *Flying Scotsman* slowly comes back to life. Eight tracks away, the Gulf Mobile & Ohio's overnight St. Louis to Chicago *Midnight Special* is nearly ready to depart. It had carried nothing but Pullman sleepers until the end of World War II, but has now been diluted with coaches. It will survive until Amtrak takes over rail passenger service in 1971.

# St. Louis to Green Bay

In which *Flying Scotsman* gets arrested, the tour's finances worsen, and Bill throws coal into *Flying Scotsman*'s tender.

Tuesday, 7 July. In a decidedly undignified departure, *Flying Scotsman* starts the trip to Chicago by being dragged out from Union Station by a Terminal Railroad Association (TRRA) SW-1 switch engine.

The office buildings of downtown St. Louis provide the backdrop as *Flying Scotsman* charges toward the Mississippi River. When the TRRA switch engine is detached a few blocks east of Union Station, *Flying Scotsman* gets to show off her new black pilot for the first time.

As seen from the observation car, *Flying Scotsman* climbs onto Merchants Bridge to cross the Mississippi River. (Photo: Joe Petric)

*Flying Scotsman* adds some smoke to an already smoggy sky. Once the train reaches the apex of Merchants Bridge, it will drop down into the Illinois farmlands. (Photo: Joe Petric)

View from the chase, somewhere in south-western Illinois. In America the railroads came before roads and so roads followed the railroad track to find the best lie of the land between A and B. It makes chasing trains a popular pursuit to this day. With Bill back on his home turf, he found chasing *Flying Scotsman* was much easier than it had been in less familiar states. It helped that the roads frequently ran parallel to the N&W tracks and close enough to keep an eye on the train through the side-view mirror. 'Objects in mirror may be closer than they appear.'

Framed between trees and grass, *Flying Scotsman* whistles for a grade crossing.

*Flying Scotsman* crosses the Sangamon River as she nears her mid-day stop in Decatur.

A large crowd greets *Flying Scotsman* at the N&W depot in Decatur. Robin Russell attends to one of the lubricators. (Photo: Joe Petric)

Just east of Decatur, *Flying Scotsman* meets an abbreviated *Wabash Cannon Ball* on its way from Detroit to St. Louis. You can't tell from looking at it, but the *Wabash Cannon Ball* was once one of the most famous trains in the country. It was named after the popular song first recorded by the Carter Family in 1929. 'From the great Atlantic Ocean to the wide Pacific shore' goes the first line – words that also describes *Flying Scotsman's* North American adventure.

Nearing Chicago's Dearborn Station, the train backs down toward 21st Street. Note the larger outline of the switch engine that is propelling *Flying Scotsman*, giving a good indication of the difference between British and American loading gauges (the height and width of rolling stock).

Santa Fe's combined Chicago to Los Angeles *Super Chief* and *El Capitan*, led by three FP-45s, has just pulled out of Dearborn Station as *Flying Scotsman*'s observation car rounds the curve at 21st Street. It was unusual for the *Super Chief* and *El Capitan* to be combined during the summer. Normally they would operate as separate trains running on the same schedule, with the *Super Chief* carrying the Pullman sleeping cars and the *El Capitan* carrying high-level coaches. In this instance the train was nineteen cars long.

In a mirror image to the way the day began in St. Louis, *Flying Scotsman* is pushed into Dearborn Station by a Chicago & Western Indiana (C&WI) RS-1. Pushing trains with the engine crew at the back is now, internationally, an unacceptable practice. Here, *Flying Scotsman* is propelled by the switcher for some miles toward the station. Nick Lord crouches in the doorway of the observation car with a walkie-talkie to help guide the engine crew.

Wednesday, 8 July. *Flying Scotsman* opens for the first of eleven days on display at Chicago's Dearborn Station. Unlike the other big cities the train had visited, Chicago doesn't have a single train station that serves all railroads. In 1970 there are six, with Dearborn being one of the smaller ones. The expected crowds of visitors will fail to appear. Bill and Randy took two days off to return to Dixon. Randy would be driving his red Volkswagon Beetle from here on out, so they'd have two cars for the rest of the tour. They dropped off their summer's worth of film to be processed and picked up a few changes of clothes before returning to Chicago. (Photo: Joe Petric)

*Flying Scotsman* shares the platforms at Dearborn Station with a privately owned open-platform observation car. In America, these private cars could be hitched to whichever trains were going your way. *Gritty Palace* was originally built as an office car for the Rock Island Railroad. Whoever owns it had a good sense of humour. The railroad name painted on the side, GNW&B, stands for 'Going Nowhere And Back'.

Friday, 10 July. Bill Wagner and Randy Imfeld take over souvenir sales on the train and immediately make some pricing and advertising changes. Davina Flint shows off a *Flying Scotsman* tea tray, a very popular item, now available at a new higher price. George Hinchcliffe's story was that Bill and Randy had to be officially employed by the train in order to sleep on Green Bay's National Railroad Museum property. A more likely explanation is that he realized that they were a bargain at the princely wages of $5 per day. Although souvenir sales improved, the train was still not generating enough income to be anywhere near self-sufficient. Alan Pegler's bank account(s) were suffering.

Tuesday, 14 July. Always the optimist, Alan Pegler surveys the modest crowd of visitors from his vantage point on *Flying Scotsman's* footplate. After closing, Alan assembled everyone in the Fireman's Rest for a pep talk. He congratulated them on a job well done in getting as far as Chicago and talked about his plans for the rest of the summer. Then Bill and Randy shuttled everyone from the nearby Midland Hotel to volunteer Tom Leaton's parents house in suburban Elmhurst for an outdoor cookout (barbecue). (Photo: Joe Petric)

THIS PROPERTY
IN THE CUSTODY
OF
JOSEPH I. WOODS
SHERIFF OF COOK COUNTY

By: _____ Deputy

Wednesday, 15 July. It's not every day that a train gets arrested. *Flying Scotsman* was impounded by Deputy Sheriff L. H. Boyd for non-payment of a publicity company debt that had been incurred the previous year in New York City. The deputy considered arresting Alan Pegler when he tore the impound notices from the Pullman carriages on the basis that they were not Pegler's property. After a few threats of lawsuits and counter-suits, things were eventually settled on Thursday. It's not every day that a train gets released from jail.

Friday, 17 July. Free at last, *Flying Scotsman* settles in for her last night in Dearborn Station. After the exhibits close tomorrow, the train will transfer to North Western Station in preparation for Sunday's run to Green Bay. Even though Bill and Randy were now gainfully employed by the train, they were still on the lookout for money-making projects. They had found an English steam recording called *TRIUMPH OF AN A-4 PACIFIC* in a downtown record store, bought out their entire inventory of twenty-four records for $1 each, and began selling them on the train for $5. Free enterprise at its best.

Saturday, 18 July. An N&W SW-9 pulls the train out of Dearborn Station. The boxcar behind the hopper contains the train's main inventory of souvenirs. Repeated shunting had slewed the contents into a souvenir landslide. A few days earlier, *Flying Scotsman's* tender had been filled by nine tons of coal from the hopper. The coaling operation was decidedly non-trivial. The only way to transfer coal under Dearborn Station's train shed was by hand, so Bill and Randy spent an afternoon pitching shovels-full of coal across the platforms from the hopper into the tender. They'd also restocked the onboard souvenir and beer supply from the boxcar. George was making sure they were earning their $5 per day. (Photo: Joe Petric)

The next leg to Green Bay meant travelling north. The seven railroads serving Dearborn Station head every direction except north. Hence *Flying Scotsman* transfers to North Western Station for her last night in Chicago. Heading back toward 21st Street, the train passes the Santa Fe coach yard on the left. On the right, and in the preceding picture and in the next, the Chicago River is spanned by a succession of spectacular structures. (Photo: Joe Petric)

As twilight settles in, *Flying Scotsman* backs the train into North Western Station under her own power after the N&W switch engine is detached. If the train was going forward instead of backward, it would reach Bill and Randy's hometown of Dixon about 100 miles down the track. (Photo: Joe Petric).

Sunday, 19 July. It's a cold and rainy morning as *Flying Scotsman* begins the 200-mile run to Green Bay's National Railroad Museum over Chicago & North Western (C&NW) trackage.

The train hosts a massive number of invited guests – National Railroad Museum dignitaries, the media, and various hangers on. Both Pullmans and the Fireman's Rest are filled, and there is even some overflow into the administration car. It was unusual for more than a handful of invited guests to ride the train between stops. This time there were too many to be comfortable. If only Alan Pegler had known that he could have sold tickets, the day's run to Green Bay would have turned a tidy profit.

*Flying Scotsman* leans into a curve somewhere north of Milwaukee.

*Above*: En route from Ashland, Wisconsin, to Chicago, C&NW's *Flambeau 400*, led by an F-7 meets *Flying Scotsman* near Green Bay. Les Richards pushes coal forward in the tender. (Photo: Joe Petric)

*Left*: *Flying Scotsman* negotiates some questionable trackage entering the National Railroad Museum grounds in Green Bay. But at least the poor track only extended for a few hundred yards – not like the hundreds of miles of bad track on the Katy.

Les Richards jokes with some young railfans as he guides the train into the National Railroad Museum. Nick Lord in his BP overalls provides an escort on the opposite side. Bad as it was, the track was probably no worse than that found in many British motive power depots.

As always, George Hinchcliffe oversees the operation. The train won't leave the museum grounds for four weeks. George was worried about the 'questionable trackage' and always had concerns about the promises that Harold Fuller made regarding how many visitors the train would attract. As a 'national' railway museum, the British train crew was expecting an institution akin to that in the UK. The mainly outdoor exhibits were poorly presented and maintained. Today, in 2023, the museum is vastly improved and funded by an education foundation.

# Green Bay to Sarnia

In which *Flying Scotsman* runs through the night, the crew go on holiday, and Bill gets deported.

*Above*: Monday, 20 July. Face to face with Union Pacific (UP) No. 4017 (4-8-8-4) Big Boy, *Flying Scotsman* looks like a toy in contrast. Not many paying customers to be seen. Green Bay isn't a big town, and the train does not generate many additional museum visitors. Ticket and souvenir sales were both far lower than anticipated – plunging to a daily low of $30. It didn't help that the train had run out of its biggest selling souvenir, *Flying Scotsman* postcards, in Chicago. Bill and Randy convinced George to have more produced, using five of their pictures from earlier in the summer. The print run of 10,000 postcards from each of the pictures would be ready in early September.

*Left*: *Flying Scotsman's* fire slowly dies down in the firebox as the train readies for a month of inactivity. Presumably, this is the only picture in existence showing *Flying Scotsman* from a vantage point atop a UP Big Boy's smokebox.

Within days, the UK crew managed to find a soccer ball. They'd play using the gap between engines as the goal. Richard couldn't find much in Green Bay to keep him amused, but Bill and Randy took him to play miniature golf and Randy took him to see the Green Bay Packers versus New York Giants in an exhibition football game. The frequent stops in play made the game very slow compared to the sort of football that Richard was used to, but he enjoyed the hot dogs!

Harry Mason, Arthur Houghton, Alan Wappat, and Gordon Pugh enjoy lunch on an idyllic summer day at the National Railroad Museum. Not all the crew members were around to enjoy the sun. Nick Lord and Bill Brand had gone home to the UK, although Nick planned to rejoin the tour in mid-August at Milwaukee. From the crew's overall morale viewpoint, the biggest loss was Mary Elaine and Shauna going home to Texas. It was unclear if they'd be coming back, to the dismay of all the eligible men.

The museum's Lake Superior & Ishpeming (LS&I) No. 24 (2-8-0) Consolidation runs short excursions on the loop line around the grounds. *Flying Scotsman's* three drivers volunteered to operate the locomotive since they were getting bored with the inactivity. Having drivers to operate the LS&I engine was nice, but it wasn't much good without firemen. So, Bill and Randy and thirteen-year-old Richard volunteered to learn the trade, and the drivers were happy to teach them. Those strong backs helped. And that's how they became very, very, very junior-grade and heavily supervised firemen.

The tourist train at the nearby Mid-Continent Railway in North Freedom offers a brief get-away for other bored crew members. That's Richard walking by the fence in the orange T-shirt holding his trusty Kodak super-8 and a box of film. Bill and Randy each had a car to drive the crew back and forth to North Freedom, but had to schedule those trips around their junior-grade fireman duties as well as the other new role they'd assumed as janitors at the museum. They'd been hired to sweep/mop/polish every night after closing for $1.50/hour. Between that, their $5/day from George, their steam recording sales, and ongoing visits to local blood banks, they found themselves generating a healthy and diverse income stream.

Sunday, 2 August. Bill Wagner, Morgan McIlwain, Randy Imfeld, and Joe Petric pump the Mid-Continent Railway's pump-car 3 miles up the hill from North Freedom to LaRue. Richard remembers this trip to North Freedom very well. Again, Bill and Randy were in *loco parentis*. As evening turned to dusk it was decided to take the pump-car to the end of the line and back. Richard hung on for dear life as those on board speculated that they were travelling at over 30 mph on the downhill return trip. (Photo: Richard Hinchcliffe)

Friday, 7 August. There were other places close to Green Bay for the crew to visit if they wanted to see something other than more steam locomotives at the Mid-Continent Railway. Les and Ena Richards are visiting the nearby Oneida Indian reservation. Les, who was seventy-two years old, was incredibly fit and supple. He had shown off his flexibility a few nights earlier when the crew had a party at the Northland Hotel where they were staying. Les opened a book of matches, placed it on the floor, and proceeded to pick it up with his teeth. Only his feet touched the floor.

After being moved for a boiler inspection, *Flying Scotsman* is put on display at a more central location within the museum. The tour train itself is separately put on display nearby but not coupled to the locomotive. *Flying Scotsman* is seen here from the observation car's Fireman's Rest. The new location made the train more visible to museum visitors, but didn't have much effect on ticket or souvenir sales. It was increasingly obvious that the 1970 tour, just like the 1969 tour, was losing money at an alarming rate.

Instead of the UP Big Boy, *Flying Scotsman* is now face-to-face with A-4 *Dwight D. Eisenhower* No. 60008 (4-6-2), another LNER import from the UK. All the UK crew were dismayed to see the condition of the A-4. It had been left outside in the blistering sun for several years. George Hinchcliffe's memoir states that Harold Fuller wanted them to steam the A-4 but they had no idea what state the boiler was in. The tubes did not look very healthy, so they declined. However, they did have a go at raising steam with the Big Boy, but after twenty tons of coal had been burned and the boiler was only warm, they gave up.

Friday, 14 August. Bill Brand had returned home to Edinburgh, so Alan Wappat breaks in newly arrived fireman Ken Day. He would soon be put to work. Alan Pegler had just arranged with the Canadian National Railway (CN) to exhibit the train at Toronto's Canadian National Exhibition, and *Flying Scotsman* would be starting the journey to Canada on Sunday. In the day's other personnel news, Mary Elaine and Shauna returned and great was the celebration! George had negotiated with their father about their pay. This precipitated a revision in the pay of Bill and Randy to $15/day, plus 1 per cent of gross souvenir sales. In the bigger financial picture, however, it meant that the train would lose even more money each day.

Saturday, 15 August. Joe Petric gets a workout polishing *Flying Scotsman's* corridor tenders in preparation for tomorrow's departure for Milwaukee. On the last legs of the 1970 tour, *Flying Scotsman* would ultimately reach as far east as Montreal, Quebec, before retracing her route through Toronto and finally closing in Niagara Falls.

Reunited with the tour train, *Flying Scotsman* raises steam hours before leaving Green Bay (Photo: Joe Petric).

Harry Mason and Arthur Houghton are in charge of making sure *Flying Scotsman* will be ready for the run to Milwaukee in the morning. (Photo: Joe Petric).

Sunday, 16 August. Getting ready to chase *Flying Scotsman* from the air. Left to right: Mary Elaine Snow, Randy Imfeld, Richard Hinchcliffe, Shauna Snow, Bill Wagner. After Mary Elaine and Shauna had returned, Bill and Randy invited them to join the rented airplane adventure. But even with their new sources of income, the cost was still well outside of their price range. George came to the rescue – he'd pay for the charter if they'd take Richard along. It was a solution that pleased everyone.

*Flying Scotsman* is almost lost in the vast farmlands of northern Wisconsin. The light airplane pilot refused to fly any lower than 500 feet. This presented an insurmountable problem for Richard, whose movie camera was ill-equipped to film at that distance from a bouncing airplane.

The tour train heads south toward Milwaukee. There's only one Pullman in the consist now since *Isle of Thanet* remained at the National Railroad Museum in Green Bay as an addition to the *Dwight D. Eisenhower* exhibit.

*Flying Scotsman's* apple green livery blends in nicely with the trees of the Wisconsin Northwoods. This was to be Bill's last photo of *Flying Scotsman* for three days. Rather than chasing, he and Randy did some fancy car shuttling the next day so they could ride the tour train from Chicago to South Bend on its only night run of the summer. This would also be their opportunity to ride the footplate. Normally, only authorized personnel were allowed while the train was underway. But the night would hide them from view, and the crew didn't mind at all. They would use the corridor tenders to take turns on the footplate for the 100-mile run.

The train crosses the Fox River on the way out of Green Bay. *Lydia* is now the only Pullman, immediately in front of the observation car. It would be reunited with *Isle of Thanet* in 1972, when George, while rescuing *Flying Scotsman* for Bill McAlpine from Alan Pegler's creditors, liaised with Harold Fuller to have it shipped back to Wisconsin. Both Pullman cars are now back in Britain with the observation car and owned by the Swanage Railway. (Photo: Joe Petric)

*Flying Scotsman* splits a pair of C&NW semaphore signals en route to Milwaukee. (Photo: Joe Petric)

Wednesday, 19 August. *Flying Scotsman* nears Lansing, Michigan. After being up all night on the run from Chicago to South Bend and selling souvenirs for a full day, Bill had splurged on a room at the Randolph Hotel where the crew was staying. Not surprisingly, he overslept and didn't catch up with the train until Lansing.

*Flying Scotsman* passes a string of autoracks (car carriers). Nearby Detroit is the centre of American automobile manufacture, and autoracks are used to ship new cars all across the country. This was back in the days when autoracks were open to the elements and people could watch the new automobile models as they passed. Today in 2023, autoracks are fully enclosed to prevent vandals from throwing rocks or cans of paint at their cargos.

Thursday, 20 August. *Flying Scotsman* passes another autorack at Durand, Michigan. The mid-day stop here will be the last before the train crosses into Canada at Sarnia, Ontario. Before entering Canada, Bill and Randy had to provide a full list of items on the train that might be sold in the country. Prior to this, no inventory had ever been taken since the train left Britain. They talked Mary Elaine and Shauna into helping them with the Customs inventory in Lansing, and so spent most of the previous night counting all the souvenirs, kegs of beer, and various spare parts in both the supply car and the train's separate boxcar.

Nat Gould, Alan Wappat, and Les Richards give the 'thumbs up' as *Flying Scotsman* pulls out of Durand. The big smiles were undoubtedly for Mary Elaine, who was chasing with Bill. The train passed through Canadian Customs easily at Sarnia, but Mary Elaine and Bill did not. Bill stupidly told the Customs officer they were employed by the train, not realizing that would mean they would need work permits. After they were deported back to Port Huron, lots of dimes and nickels disappeared into a gas station's pay phone before they were finally connected to the hotel where the crew was staying. Somehow George managed to convince Customs to let them cross the border, even without work permits. Welcome to Canada!

# Sarnia to Niagara Falls

In which *Flying Scotsman* shows off her speed, Alan Pegler makes some efficiencies, and Richard sneaks back to America.

Friday, 21 August. Maybe not back in the UK but at least back on Commonwealth rails, *Flying Scotsman* blasts across western Ontario on the way to Toronto. The train will be on display at the Canadian National Exhibition (CNE) until 8 September. The CNE is an annual event that lasts for eighteen days at the end of the summer. It's a gigantic celebratory fair with agricultural and science exhibits, sporting events, live music, and a sampling of food from across the country.

The train passes a grain elevator as it nears Toronto. Although it looks like a rural scene, there are commuter trains that serve this small station. *Flying Scotsman* will be parked on the CNE grounds by the end of the day.

*Right*: Davina Flint poses with a *Flying Scotsman* souvenir beneath the shadow of the Gardiner Expressway at the very edge of the CNE grounds where the train is parked. This poor location guarantees that ticket and souvenir sales will be less than expected. There's a story behind the souvenir that Davina was holding. The original price had been 5 cents, with very few being sold. When Bill and Randy took over souvenir sales in Chicago, they christened them 'Alumo-Prints' and raised the price to $1. They began to sell at a respectable pace – but it was still just a drop in the bucket compared to the rate at which the train was haemorrhaging money.

Thursday, 3 September. Just in time to go on sale for a few days at the CNE, the long-awaited *Flying Scotsman* replacement postcards finally arrive. Bill had written the captions for the postcards to mimic the grandiloquent authorship of the famed railroad photographers Lucius Beebe and Charles Clegg. The caption for the postcard on the far right reads: 'Bursting through a dense, pre-Cambrian morass, *Flying Scotsman* appears as some antediluvian behemoth raging through the primordial moraine region of southern Wisconsin. Phase II of its USA tour Slaton, Texas to Green Bay, Wisconsin – is almost completed on this wet, murky July 19th, 1970.' The postcards sell well. (Photo: Bill Gamble)

*Left*: By chance, Harry Mason is reunited with a former LNER driver who has retired to Toronto. Bill will accidentally become a very, very, very junior-grade driver. George had started selling footplate rides up and down the 300 yards of track between the now-detached exhibition cars and the end of the siding. One day Bill was sitting in the driver's seat talking to the driver, Gordon Pugh, when a customer appeared. Gordon said, 'Take it away, Bill.' Bill had seen enough to more or less know what to do and managed to get *Flying Scotsman* up and down the track without serious damage to either the locomotive or the CNE grounds.

*Below*: Tuesday, 8 September. Leaving the Canadian National Exhibition behind, *Flying Scotsman* heads east toward Ottawa, the capital of Canada. The track is good and *Flying Scotsman* enjoys some high-speed running up to 75 mph.

Eastbound for Ottawa, a distant *Flying Scotsman* meets a westbound CN 'Turbotrain' on the Toronto–Montreal corridor. The 'Turbotrains' were 100 mph experimental gas turbines that were being tested in both the US and Canada. With *Flying Scotsman* sometimes operating at 75 mph here, it's possible that the closing speed for this meeting neared 175 mph.

Wednesday, 9 September. *Flying Scotsman* shares the grounds of the Canada Science and Technology Museum just south of downtown Ottawa with CN No. 6200, (4-8-4) Northern on permanent display.

Thursday, 10 September. Les Richards gets his hands dirty with the never-ending maintenance on *Flying Scotsman*. Les and the firemen were perpetually busy keeping *Flying Scotsman* in running order, but staffing requirements for the tour train itself had been dropping since Kansas City. The 1 per cent of gross souvenir sales that Bill was being paid totalled $26 for the previous two weeks – which meant an average daily sales total of less than $200. Even having only two people staffing the souvenir table had become an unnecessary extravagance.

*Flying Scotsman* still isn't attracting big crowds, but at least a few school groups visit now. The financial pinch of running the tour comes to a head. Within days, Alan Pegler will take the necessary step of downsizing the staff. Gordon and Ethyl Pugh, Arthur Houghton, Alan Wappat, and Davina Flint will be on their way back to the UK. And the Snow sisters, Mary Elaine and Shauna, will be on their way back to Texas. Bill wouldn't be around to see these changes as School (as university is called in America) was back in session. He was leaving the next day to return to Illinois for his senior year at Bradley University.

Saturday, 12 September. Before his mother could say no, Richard tagged along with Bill, Randy, and Nick Lord to chase New York Central and St. Louis (Nickel Plate Road) No. 759 (2-8-4), from Harrisburg to Gallitzen, Pennsylvania. For Richard, this would be the highlight of his American adventure. He and Nick had driven down with Randy on Friday, while Bill had detoured on his way back to Illinois. The train ran on both Saturday and Sunday, so Nick and Richard rode it one day and chased it with Bill and Randy the next. Meanwhile, *Flying Scotsman* had migrated eastward 123 miles to Montreal.

Sunday, 13 September. Penn Central's New York to Pittsburgh *Duquesne* passes No. 759 on the 12-mile, one in seventy gradient through Horseshoe Curve to Gallitzen. On the right, an eastbound freight led by an SD-45 and a U30C drifts down the mountain. Richard and Nick are getting a spectacular dose of big-time American railroading. Bill went back to college, and two days later Randy called him from the train to tell him about the downsizing. Randy did not mention that all of his cameras, film and Richard's movie camera had been stolen from his car overnight after they had rejoined *Flying Scotsman* in Montreal.

Thursday, 1 October. *Flying Scotsman* is on display at Hamilton's Canadian National Railway Station. After venturing as far east as Montreal, the train has steamed back through Toronto and is now one stop away from the 1970 tour's termination in Niagara Falls, Ontario. Bill had cut three days' worth of classes to return for the tour's last days of exhibiting. He couldn't pass up the chance to chase *Flying Scotsman*'s last run of the summer, and say good-bye to his friends on the crew.

A cameraman from one of Hamilton's TV stations films George Hinchcliffe and Alan Pegler in deep discussion while Richard Hinchcliffe, minus his super-8 movie camera, is now left with just his tape recorder.

*Above*: This is the backbone of *Flying Scotsman's* skeleton crew: Ken Day (only remaining fireman), Nat Gould (only remaining driver), Les Richards, and George Hinchcliffe. They'll be responsible for taking *Flying Scotsman* the remaining 45 miles to Niagara Falls in the morning.

*Right*: But before that last run to Niagara Falls, Nat Gould was presented with the 'Grand Master of the Wooden Spoon'. It was awarded to Nat on the basis that he was the 'heavy driver,' the one particular member of the crew that bumped the train the most when setting off. It is more likely that Alan Pegler actually deserved the award, but Nat was very genial and good natured about it. 'You rascals, you,' he said. 'I'll mount the 'diploma' and wooden spoon on a wall back home.'

Friday, 2 October. *Flying Scotsman* rolls toward Niagara Falls, the last stop on the tour. The exhibits will be open through 6 October before the 1970 tour is officially shut down.

Backing toward CN's Niagara Falls station, Alan Pegler takes over the throttle from Nat Gould. Only one could be the real 'heavy driver'.

Alan Pegler's daughter Penny and Simon Puser enjoy the view from the administration car as the train approaches Niagara Falls. Penny had joined the train at Chicago, helping out wherever and whenever needed. Simon had managed the train's money since Slaton. At least when it came to ticket and souvenir sales, bookkeeping seemed somewhat less than rigorous. Sales were never matched against inventory – there wouldn't even have been an inventory if the train hadn't entered Canada. And money from the sales of *TRIUMPH OF AN A-4 PACIFIC* was co-mingled with the train's money. In the end it probably didn't matter. It was just a question of how long Alan would keep paying the bills out of his own pocket.

The crowds that had greeted *Flying Scotsman* earlier in the summer are replaced by a single piper as the train arrives in Niagara Falls.

Saturday, 3 October. The stairs are in place and the flags are flying, but there are no visitors in sight. During the summer of 1970 *Flying Scotsman* has travelled approximately 3,400 miles and been seen by perhaps a million people both as visitors to the train and at trackside. Unfortunately, only the former had generated revenue. (Photo: Joe Petric)

Evening closes in on *Flying Scotsman* as the 1970 tour comes to an end. The train will eventually be moved to Toronto to spend the winter in CN's Spadina roundhouse before the 1971 journey to San Francisco. This will be in the further unsuccessful pursuit of British government backing and corporate sponsorship. But that'll be a story for someone else to tell. Bill and Randy left the train the next day and convoyed back across Canada and into the US. Bill would be back in classes on Monday, and Randy would be on his way to Texas. Richard meanwhile, was back at school in Lincolnshire grappling with culture shock.

# Epilogue

*Right*: Weddings, Part I. For most of the crew, the summer of 1970 was just an enjoyable, educational, and entertaining episode in their lives. But for four of them, it was life altering. The eligible men from the UK side of the pond were train managers Nick Lord and Ron Hawkes. Ron always had a thing for Mary Elaine but Randy would eventually become the chosen man. Nick married Shauna.

*Below*: Weddings, Part II. Bill Wagner and Randy Imfeld represented the American side of the eligible men on the train. Randy and Mary Elaine got married several years after the tour but subsequently divorced.

Reunions, Part I. Saturday, 5 August, 2017. While on holiday in England, Bill and his wife Barbara accidentally came across *Flying Scotsman* at York's National Railway Museum. Even though she had been 'un-Americanized' and was now as she was in British Railways days, (no headlight, no bell, no pilot, elephant ear smoke deflectors and renumbered from 4472 to 60103) Bill recognized it immediately. *Flying Scotsman* would be pulling an excursion train from York to Carlisle via Leeds and Skipton the next day. Bill worked in Information Technology before retiring in 2007. He and Barbara live in Austin, Texas.

Reunions, Part II. Thursday, 12 May 2022. Richard sits above *Flying Scotsman's* buffer beam in a re-creation of the scene in St Louis from 4 July, 1970. Below from left to right are Lee Kenny, Colin Green, and Sharoon Yousaf. The engine is at Bury in the hands of Riley and Sons who will be re-tubing the boiler. The war in Ukraine has delayed efforts to source tubes and fittings, but *Flying Scotsman* should be running again in 2023 in time to celebrate her 100th birthday. Richard worked in higher education but is now retired and lives with his wife Catherine in Cumbria. (Photo: Bill Gamble)